Marine Layer

Marine Layer

Kit Robinson

BLAZEVOX[BOOKS]
Buffalo, New York

Marine Layer
by Kit Robinson
© 2015 by Kit Robinson. All rights reserved.
Published by BlazeVOX [books]

Printed in the United States of America

Interior design and typesetting by Geoffrey Gatza
Cover art by Kit Robinson

First Edition
ISBN: 978-1-60964-229-7
Library of Congress Control Number: 2015948505

BlazeVOX [books]
131 Euclid Ave
Kenmore, NY 14217
Editor@blazevox.org

publisher of weird little books

BlazeVOX [books]

blazevox.org

21 20 19 18 17 16 15 14 13 12 01 02 03 04 05 06 07 08 09 10

BlazeVOX

Acknowledgments

Big thanks to Ted Pearson, Ted Greenwald and Geoffrey Gatza.

Some of these poems have appeared in *Across the Margin, Annex Press, Banqueted, Dreamboat, Ladowich, Memory is a Kind of Accomplishment, Oversound, Poetry is Dead, Prelude, Sprung Formal, The Recluse* and *VLAK.*

for Tom Raworth

CONTENTS

Irish Beach 13
57 Varieties 13
Those Recently Met 17
Running on Empty 19
Marine Layer 21
The Idea Takes Time 26
10 Things 27
No Such Thing as Silence 28
Destroyed Work 30
Transistor Radio 32
Eventual Lispector 34
Turn on All the Receivers 36
The Corporation Yard 38
Construction Is the Love of Coffee 40
Cloudy and Cool at the Car Wash 41
Nights Flicker, Feelings Well Up 42
In the Curvature of the Moment 43
Several Seconds Later Another Letter 45
Neighboring Vessels 48
Signal Strength 51
States of Mind Fit Together 53
Put a Notebook on the Nightstand 54
This Written Record Is an Enclosure 55
Rhythm of the Logs 56
High Dudgeon 57
The Something that Comes out of Nothing 59
Familiar Faces under Soft Lights 60
Construction is the Noise of Spring 62
Time is What We are Given 65
Relaxin' at Yorkville 67
Mistakes Are Normal 70
No Time like the Right Time 73
Dreams Are as Real as We Are 75
Far Be It from Me 77
The Turnstile of the Present 78
Where Here We Grind 79
In My Guise 81
A Transom Window 83

The Line in the Sand 86
The Poem Is a Reversible Jacket 88
Daydreaming in Icelandic 89
We Keep Saying They Though She Is Gone 91
The Dandelions Are Out Again This Morning 93
The Sky Is White Because It's Fog 95
The Star Inside the Rock..97
Walking and Talking..98
What a Beautiful Thing...100
Internal Combustion 102
For Selling Cigarettes? 104
Lane Shipping 106
A Stone's Throw 108
Like Birds in Air...110
Every Time We Say Goodbye 112
Raspberries in January 114
Unconfirmed Reports 116
Master Class... 117
The Avenue of Kisses 119
An Old Signature.. 121
Stars over Mongolia... 124
Weather.. 126
The Lost Steps 128
The Rose Quartet 130

Marine Layer

IRISH BEACH

Satellite dish picks up signals
Part for the whole
Sound waves ocean jetliner

Similar to drink of water
Cleanses the Paleolithic

Local color is gray
Non-specific waves thru fog
Enter two bikes

The way south is strewn
Falls over onto the side of talk

Somewhere between landscape
Ampersand portrait
Art hugs the coastline

Car door closes on air
Chew on time

There is a football field of it
In every direction
Dark undersides of leaves

Psychological hummingbird
The clock strikes Great Horned Owl

Fog strokes the coast
Build local shake back into place
Hire contractors to write this

Message in light breeze
Animal action elsewhere

Load up on little color
Some pink there
A bit of orange

Establish ongoingness of objects
Sandals comma hand weights comma

Driftwood like whale or arm
Mind drifts until big truck
Can't see waves at moment

Similar to being on slow
Think thru combination of things

Page flips in wind
Motorcycle monograph day
Up or down hill all

Right at edge
Hear almost everything else

THOSE RECENTLY MET

Derogatory apartments
No sentence unlasted
Differences scratch bottom
A whether of doubts
Table tennis to the jars

In plain representatives
The skins of apples are repaired
By the blind surrealist
Cooped up all these years
Like it or not

Go hungry and multiply
It only takes a few minutes
Lives unfold like camp chairs
The story of the story
Fire in the belly of the beast

Patterns print generations
Out of whole cloth
Dream narrative makes better sense
Echoes arrive early
Do voices echo thought?

Each tribe makes its own breakfast
Ladders are propped against buildings or put away
Thumbs up if by sea
Cross currents etch the surface
Essentials unwind into common sense

Those recently met
The roadside installation artist
The lighting technician

The proprietress
The ceramicist farmer

People not otherwise encountered
Full of life of place
Landscape with hawk and sparrow
Roads pointing this way and that
Limits to what can be said or done

Such imaginary orange boundaries
Stand in for gaping fear
About face
The dawn tingles
Syllables drop like weights

Interior space is deep
Empty as eyes in a blink
Charged particles give off heat
Faster than thought
The community is cool

The road is narrow
The situation is normal
All fucked up
Yet perfectly fine
Well which is it?

RUNNING ON EMPTY

Lift the situation off its face
Under cycle not known at this time
Seriously didn't know that
Explore tree-lined grottoes
Wait, that can't be
Over the shoulder remnants tow a wake
Become ok
Lead underwater legions to the light
Not commenting on anything right now
Burrow into hole in time

Running on empty
The sky is beautiful
Goes without saying
When I see the glory
Become ok
Be along in a minute
Somebody bouncing a basketball one yard over
Why wait?
Each thing comes with its color
The life is full of them

Ellingtoniana
Allusions to the cresting of Harlem
Drum battles at 4:38
Morning is afternoon
Water on television
When did you become so strong?
Wait for plot to catch up
Bass player is mad cool
Music via window
Get your ticket at said station

You have the patience of a *santo*
Buy the next rhomboid
Cloud the shape of an elephant west to east
Now clear sky as far as the eye can sleep
Awake to a posse of hill dwellers
This speech is inside out

MARINE LAYER

Marine layer
Top of the morning
Familiar ring

Lost in thought
A percentage of
Off and running

You hold the key
Time to go

They also serve
Stand and deliver

Chopping block
Time and time
Serious ladies

Arm around
When in the course
Open the gate

Swivel hips
Likely story

Dead by rights
Certain to impress

A nice feel
Built from scrap
Smoke at sunset

Imagine this
Nothing but space
Light emanates out

Captured in crystals
Too weak to hold

They break
Spilling everything

That hurts
Truth in fragments
On uneven ground

Your job
Repair the damage

A little today
The wide world

Come into focus
Light the lights
Gather here

Simply marvelous
Hi-de-ho
Clever comedians

This rough magic
Characteristic

On the cuff
Off the clock

Sun comes through
Touches a nerve
Speaks volumes

Tribal reports
Deep in studio time
The song is handsome

Writing you a letter
When the air brightens

No trees in forest
Only words

They sometimes say
What cannot be said
Or so we thought

Come to find out
There's gold in them
There in the hills

Chunks of meaning
Fall through fingers

Rough integers
Without number

The joy of it all
Get to see
Get to listen

Ecstatic angles
Mondrian floor
Cat on a homemade fence

Interruption rings
Cup-and-saucer tingle

Buzz-saw day
Like it or not

Nothing more important
Get to work
Sorting flames

Universal joint
Sky sail common
Sympathetic vibe

World full to bursting
Hands on deck

Much as like
Size fits all

Something missing
Too much of a thing
Good on you

Thanks a lot
See you in the middle
Biding our time

The breeze stirs
The leaves sway

Electric training
Think and be thunk

THE IDEA TAKES TIME

To write these words as if someone else
Would be a pleasure the quick release
Perhaps possible as each is multiple
Not knowing how things will turn out
Until the fumble end of any oxcart
Bumps down the road to one front porch
After another has pulled up stakes
Light at the end of the tunnel turning on
Life in batches mixed with strong air
A line of thinking straight to the heart of matter

Don't forget to breathe while drinking coffee
The next instant a wild caribou how to connect
Fabulous organizations print money in midnight cathedrals
Simplicity favors the blonde in the pin-striped idea
Late comers bunch up in alternative tea-room vantage points
So long in coming so loathe to go
A paraphrase of World War II
Kicking up sparks on the road to Tucumcari
You think you know where you are and are wrong again
This sense of displacement is vaguely familiar

The idea takes time to grow from seed to flower
Meanwhile you live and it's not just for humids anymore
Stand at attention outside the gate
Brandish complexity the subject is not white
Not black, not red, not green, is virtually colorless
Changing light bulbs inside and out
It would be very nice to be here again
The banks are muddy that hold the rapid times
A painter captures light on water time of day
A song the only point of contact rushing home to meet them

10 THINGS

A rusted cloud
A drowsy ball
A still branch
A carved stack
A simple corner
A crazed glass
A pretty total
A lost move
The sorry situation
The brilliant door

NO SUCH THING AS SILENCE

Unhook cause and effect
No matter how many stars are being queried
Does not currently support augmented reality
Conditioner logic, if/then & null
Absolute object placement

Daily life is bumpy enough as it is
The moon is hidden the marine layer thick
Verification principle rinse and repeat
Things happen for multiple reasons
Who have no time for poetry

Wash nature off the back of time
Ontic handles present themselves freely
Sunny olive state to big bamboo
The city a kind of virtual prose
Neither smooth nor vascular in its prolonged crevices

Barking dog a marker for the present moment
I don't care what we go with as long as we are consistent
Things are at our disposal
Crazy words with no meaning don't listen to them
Let us repair to the garden of earthly delights

Something is something like nothing from the oven
Dashboards are embeddable
We need to loop in Hubert
I'm dappled and drowsy and ready for sleep
No such thing as silence

Thanks for driving this piece
Over an open field
Manual transmission chrome wheels
Hammer sounds punctuate the sentence
The voice of the planet is heard in the land

DESTROYED WORK
For Andrew Joron

I dreamed Lamantia showed me his secret book
It opened from the top, was old, like a photo album and stuffed
Full of small things, papers, like matchbooks or bubble gum commix
That represented jokes, private parties, parting shots
A reliquary of sorts, caught between shakes and the ecstatic

A paper bull, the piñata of a long forgotten child's birthday, swings
    wildly from a string
Stretched taut between tree and shed
His snout a disaster of snakes jiggling candy
Ears blowing smoke tail flipping air in an unimaginably broken
    background
As the foreground too is torn to shreds in the morning after

Images salute the day
By how many particulars must we address this simple October rectory
Bad language takes us by the hand and samples us
Until the life of stems irrigates the flowers of our uncertain prospects
It's a bumpy ride, yet propitious

Whereas the refusal by certain Congressmen to fund the government
Do not assume for a minute that midnight lives
In a car once occupied by John Wieners
When he was trying to get permission to return to Boston
His arm and hammer have remained there since notwithstanding the
    bothersome efforts of tattling press agents

Locomotion is good for you
Crack open the *matrioshka* of circular thinking
Eisenstein taught us to edit against the grain
Neither arm seems attached to the body of work
Thus literature flies in the face of public opinion

Something is missing, a pineapple
I cling to my residence like a simile
I imagine the symbolic to be real
And vice versa
All dreams are dreams in name only

On the ocean floor a sudden squirt of saliva
Awakens the surly beast
Things fall apart before one has had a chance to see what they even are
Yes, we are on, but the dates and times keep changing
You look forward to open your heart to the wind and rain

Calamitous encounters, songs played at the wrong speed
Doors open into room after room each prepared for another ghost
Terrible battles over rebar
Housing starts mounted on a wall
The tall, slender reeds in a delta deciding what to do

And in this year the cockatoo
Spills seeds from its cage into news feeds bulging with fright
Prepositional logic has no apposite
The mind bends around the image of a tree
To get to the other side

I dreamed I stepped off the top of a mountain
And floated high above a mountainous landscape
Green with repetition
Until my feet touched down on a city building top
But I had become oversized, my shoes covered most of the roof

TRANSISTOR RADIO

Transistor radio
Baseball still the game
Time flows
Iceberg lettuce remember
You're tuned into

Tip o' the cap
Diamond sutra
Military miniature
Line of sight
Bring the heavy guns

Almost all women
Poll the band
Marxist poppies
I'm the opposite
See you at Juan's place

Let out the clutch
Stand up sit down guy
Balfour goes to work
Will call you at 2
The day at speed

The benches empty
No punches thrown
Nothing to speak of
Unhook, unhook and go
It doesn't take much

Time for a shower
Hit the road
Bottom of the ninth

Sky is blue
Earth our ancestral home

EVENTUAL LISPECTOR
for Laynie Browne

Awake, a week
Noli me tangere
Snooze, you lose
Bank on it
Brisk air, hello

No wind as of yet
Open for business
Sitting up straight
The best you can do
Little else interests us

Marks on wax
Right from the start
Put a pillow case
Horns are a stumbling block
Sabbaticals are ok

Wrestle with coffee
Book goes deep
A long look
Abandon all jook
Who enter jive

Parenthetical sleeves
The mind is lazy
No business sense
Late bloomer
New century

Game is mañana
Play to win
An obvious question
Where's the medicine
Banana Republican death grip

Interesting analogy
We think by walking
The store is open
The walls, plastered
Everyone eats outside

Let the poem breathe
Girls get sweaty and dirty
Happy to simply be
Light strikes up the day
Make your own heat

What we get to
Is going to
Do not hesitate to call
Nice note from you
Thanks for heads up

She writes what she thinks
Feels right at the time
Time to go
As always
Unencumbered, shoving off

TURN ON ALL THE RECEIVERS

Turn on all the receivers
Get Marx out of mothballs
Who can run fast
And lacerate the situation while standing
The picture wants a frame

Territory lights sparkle out of range
Millions of emails say the same thing
It's easy floating in a flat-bottomed boat
Don't park in a bus stop
The name of the color is twilight blue

We could go on like this for a long time
Temporary shelter on a beach
Let's hear it for the pre-conscious
Poetry is tomorrow
Leaning into the wind

Thank you thank you let's shake on it
Our polis a sum of agreements
God is unbelievable
Simply assumed by tribal lore
We share spares at the electron shop

Things to do: make list
A walk to the post office is a breath of fresh air
Memory waves on stems of self assurance
The past absorbs us
The future a ticket to ride

What can be done differently will be
It's only a matter of time
The earth in crisis

Who will lend a hand to repair
Simple situations are never that simple

Build out the implications of desire
Retrieve existential putty
Who among us has time to spare
Does most good to sit up straight and listen
The phone will ring how soon

THE CORPORATION YARD
for Ahni Robinson

And so I put my puns in order
Seeing as everything means something else
Our mouths filled with blah blah blah
A rear view camera keeps the past from getting too close
All the stores are closed but the town is thriving

Stop and take a picture where that place used to be
Where you slept in a tree house
Cold in February
Serpentine cliff face green straight down into river
Patches of snow, muddy boots, call of the schoolyard

See your breath in black and white and Technicolor
Put words in your bath
Be the same boy or girl you were before you got here
Your face before your parents were born
Keep your eye out for horn players

High bridge low water orange foliage
On the burnt slopes
New construction booming
The fact of the matter is
Where the river meets the road

Who doesn't keep her horses penned
No one likes this
We met them walking down the road
And stayed in a rusted trailer
The political arm of earth

Foggy along the coast a conversation
Vines dying back in the valleys

Talk of dams, water rights, peoples, power, farms, fish
The clock winds down on memory
Today is a shovel

Get cleaned up real good
Make lists, walk streets, size things up
Fulfill the requirements
Leave things out
Pick up supplies on way back

A concerted literalism
Penetrates the day
Moving large and small matters into place
As the sun somewhere behind gray sky the limit
Moves secretly westward in the direction of Japan

CONSTRUCTION IS THE LOVE OF COFFEE
for Alli Warren

She is so much better
So I have to be that much milder
She is the young poet
Every line she writes comes from somewhere else
All hung together
On the scaffolding of her appetite
As she strides out into this world
As she strides out into this sorry world
Take it outside and beat it with a stick
The next thing you know is English

Lights on inside and out
I.e., the sun, the sun and the overhead
The stand lamp and the desk lamp
The cool air refreshing the page
Light on a box of books
Inside the pen no thoughts
Does the salmon have a penis?
No, silly! The fishermen look to see
Nothing pushes or pulls from the past or future
Hammer sounds round out the neighborhood

Construction is the love of coffee
It's ok to talk to yourself
Time passes itself
At the crossroads
Elegua! Elegua! We salute you!
The trees of the forest are not more beautiful than this
A cool wind ruffles the lower branches
We assemble here for this game of birth and death
Oh Elegua! Saint Christopher bearing the Child on his shoulder
Across the River of Time a palm staff in his other hand

CLOUDY AND COOL AT THE CAR WASH

Cloudy and cool at the car wash
Fog moving in
Fall leaves you no other choice
The whoosh of tires
A few drops

Mild honk in mid-sentence
Pair of girls walk by
Dad passes football to son
Daughter runs to catch up
As across the street they go

Wish I had a hoodie
The season is definitely turning
Dude in dreds on skateboard
Here's my car now
Two guys with rags wipe it down

NIGHTS FLICKER, FEELINGS WELL UP

Days go by, thoughts flicker
Too much and not enough
Wings self-image down to the water
Vulnerability two-time space capsule red shift
Boy-type feelings in the man
The information overload hit record proportions
Wrong word, wrong place, wrong time
Bits scattered about on the floor
Said consciousness is off said hook
Peeling off layers of industry

Long grain rice
Temperamental upheaval
Everything is slightly oof
Before you do something, chew something
Listening to echoes in the heart
Sound coming from misdirections
Perfect nature laid out to dry
Click every integer into place
Temper metal noodles
In happy skull pan

Nights flicker, feelings well up
Neither here nor there
An image of flight, a body of water
Tenderness written by hand
Sensitivity extant over time
Selected data
Spot on, right here, now playing
A room suffused with light
Being aware, engaged
Separations employed to effect

IN THE CURVATURE OF THE MOMENT

In the curvature of the moment
A big surprise
Like a ton of bricks
A manner of speaking
All dressed up
No time like the right time
Across 110th Street
A decided advantage
Swing for the trees
Look both ways before crossing

The crossing guard was old
You can't prepare for it
Snuck in through bent bars
As expected
Standing in a hole
Light as a feather
Lined with rubble
The distraction of fathers in letters
People get ready
Come as you are

You will totally go far
Down steps into woods
Waiting for a train
She does her homework right away
I'll tell you more later
A high notch is a crow's nest
Paving the way for development
The future tense
A gigantic aircraft carrier
On the other side of the world

While here at home
You look out your window
See the cat on the fence
Sky is overcast
Relaxed and alert
Expecting a call
Loosely prepared
Get to the point
Lost in thought
I look forward to seeing you there

SEVERAL SECONDS LATER ANOTHER LETTER

Hit a speed bump
When in London
Psychic ratatouille
Swing legs over edge of bed
Wind up in hospital
Narrative cabin pressure
Life in a sunny place
All manner of imaginings
Truly freely safe
A cardboard box to hide in

The author hides behind her words
Maximum leeway to play
Minimum street imposition
Rule-based game theory night
Counting the cards of a brilliant philosophical order
Shine on Harley-Davidson
A challenger brand in a rapidly growing market
Once you do something it's done
How many times have I told you
The border is squiggly

No one knows what this is
The message reaches across time
The rhythm of speech a carrier frequency recognizable somewhere
Standing on the high board
Our work is poised at the Front
Not knowing what will come next
And so on for any number of years
Until a catch in the voice
Registers emotion
All the way down in the belly

That they are fragile
That they can go away
That they are absorbed in something right now
Busy with work, travel, complications
Busy with sorrow
That they are teeming with life
That they are conflicted
That they will stick by their commitment
Walking alone across the mostly empty parking lot

The wide sea
The gentle caress
The hairpin turn
The favorite horse
The ticking clock
The hairdresser's son
The happy warrior
Angles on affability
Possibilities for relationship
To be connected later

The reader is listening for something else
A way out
A way in
Sense data spread wide
Bright physical character in full bloom
Neither will she say anything about it
Nor will she show up to class
The rain is a figment of doubt
Trailing the open letter
Caught on the coattails of the century

What would happen if we just kept going
No locks on the doors
No break for lunch

No down time in the trailer
Keep the cameras rolling
We can edit this later
Thanks in part to a basketball
Not forgetting a drum set
Make sure the dolls are tucked in their beds
Childhood continues without us

Several seconds later another letter
Sound travels faster from ear to eye
Mixed up thoughts stand for a person
The sidewalk is full of them
Baby-carriage taxi pick-up truck bike
The great vehicle and the lesser vehicle
Standing still for long periods of time
Wide awake when not fast asleep
Somewhere in between the local butcher
And the one who supplies the juice

NEIGHBORING VESSELS
for Brandon Brown, C.S Giscombe and Carla Harryman

Um, hi
There is a class divide in my neighborhood
The fake bunny never moves
Messianic capillaries branch out
A dissonance of developments

Petit bourgeois homeowners vs. Section 8 renters
Crazy Chester followed me and he caught me in the 21st century
It is our job to repair the fractured sprocket holes of time
Some like making lists, others prefer to label buckets
Uh, thanks for coming out

Walt Disney based Main Street on his sketches of Prague, 1954
Fireworks simulate the breaking of cosmic vessels by emanations of the
    infinite
Thought is sometimes problem-solving, sometimes the posing of
    questions
I know you could have done a lot of other things
While one group sees property in terms of improvement, the other goes
    outdoors to socialize, smoke and talk trash

Job said, "Wisdom comes into being out of nothing," because thought
    does not grasp it
Rumor has it theory is baked in
For reasons which I will explain at the after-party
Incommensurate cultures continue to inhabit contiguous space
Matty told Hatty about a thing she saw, had two big horns and a wooly
    jaw

Is writing a vessel for thought?
I'm just gonna say this
A tree fell on my car while I was driving

The book Rick's "book club" is not reading this week is …
If one person humiliates you and another honors you, are the two equal
    in your eyes?

This part is already online
The street is a common denominator, now covered with debris
Five businessmen, ten empty wine glasses, at table in a Plexiglas
    enclosure, all fondling their devices (consulting their phones)
Begin to combine letters, a few or many, permuting and revolving them
    rapidly until your mind warms up
The plenitude of dimensions explodes the Cartesian grid

 "Survival requires fluency in two or more of the five sacred tongues of
    seeing"
Carl had a call scheduled for midmorning Hawaii time at boot camp
    while searching for a snack in his sleep
The world that is coming is light on branches, insight into shadows of
    leaves
Thought reaches a state of equilibrium through a process of continuous
    selection
This is a poem for Wanda Coleman

Carl sells himself his own name and keeps the change
Knowing comes out of nowhere
Form the letters carefully and we will find out what you think
All Gaul is divided into three partitas
What gets left out, and its shadow question, *who* gets left out

Me: "I always felt like she was kinda outta touch with reality"
John Rapko: "Reality doesn't like to be touched"
A week goes by there's almost nothing to it
A life goes by the archive is buried in snow
Apollinaire: "Cavalry bridges nights livid with alcohol"

More information, more entropy, more uncertainty, more freedom

I, uh, yeah, um, heh heh
A fan swished a half-court shot to win a 70-inch TV
Joni parked in front of our house since the fire trucks were blocking hers
Traces of light adhere to the shattered vessels

SIGNAL STRENGTH

Told simply
Another story
Interrupted often
Hadn't known
Tension doorway
Super interested
Recording device
The insect mind
Totally doubt
Going next

In the bag
Argue again
Whole family
Not there
Rules of conduct
Abandoned dreams
Still alive
Exert influence
Parenthetical
Pressure cooker

Night release
Battered trees
Storm drain
Cleanup crew
Not watching
Signal strength
Surgical strike
Rhyming fool
Love letter
Poet's walk

In the meanwhile
Schedule good
Tyrant hydrant
About-face day
Not nearly
Enter early
Borrowed time
Club dates
Circular system
Offshore rocks

Batting zero
Sparrow tats
Bus-side glory
Way with works
Combo fever
Empty arsenal
Brisk walk
Hand jive
Carbon footprint
Latter day

STATES OF MIND FIT TOGETHER

States of mind fit together
Like a jigsaw puzzle of gerrymandered territories
Belonging to parties mutually opposed
Until such time as joint enmity against a third-party threat
Brings them together at which point their agreement
Constitutes a new reality, one equipped with a fully functioning kitchen
Pleasant odors drift off to the side room
Where workers and friends hang out during holidays
Their children playing on the steps
The branches of the trees bare witness to the whiteness of the sky

PUT A NOTEBOOK ON THE NIGHTSTAND

Put a notebook on the nightstand
The better to remember your dreams
They slip away in the morning light
Flash shows of eerie intimacy
Viewed from the deck
Of an icebound exploration
Expert at leaving things out

THIS WRITTEN RECORD IS AN ENCLOSURE

This written record is an enclosure
Keeping out what's not said
The aches and pains, the chill factor
The sudden dread, the regrets
The unobtainable, the just missed
The nervous hankering for the next fix
All that isn't, putting pressure on whatever is
While inside the letters float from word to word
In uneven distribution like clapping sounds heard
Inside the house or out on the hazy street at the very least

Can you feel this passion, this zeal?
The way it makes a corner, turns the dial?
Breads a cutlet, skins a rabbit?
Makes way for ducklings?
Posits a better world, wanders off stage?
Wonders about this one, how to adapt?
Whether to break in half?
There is every reason to believe
A loose combination of conscious and unconscious rudiments
Will tell you all you need to know, and then some

RHYTHM OF THE LOGS
for Jack Collom

It's a wide wide wide wide world
Human consciousness is neither here nor there
Read the tree leaves
Big airport near giant mountain range
Which is which?
Rhythm of the logs
An account of being planted, watered, growing, changing with the
    seasons, enduring, providing shade, being looked at, being
    unnoticed, housing birds, bugs and other organisms, fungus, mold,
    covered in snow, swaying in the wind, being cut down, milled and
    used in construction, standing still for long periods of time, growing
    rings inside with age, being one of many, dying, return to earth, join
    universe, uninterrupted flux, food for poets, angular upright offering
More and more people arrive and depart
At a macro level everything goes on as usual
An amalgam of crises building up steam to achieve equilibrium

HIGH DUDGEON
for Will Alexander

Seeing stars in the backs of cabs the green and yellow wristband of Orula
    flashes peripheral vision
Alternate universes flex a revolving door in circulatory seminal night
Explosions rock the Crimea robins come to light on fence posts in Paris,
    Kentucky
We can go to Mexico can't we? The serious bars are open to our
    penetrating irascible thirst
How extravagant the wash of tides on the beaches of West Africa now
    where did I put that notebook?
Even infinitesimal organic infusoria color the waters off Argentina the so
    called red snow
Where oh where will the repetitious inferences of unremitting
    bureaucrats finally come to rest?
What wolves are these that pair our eyes streaming in the afterglow a
    long way from the first death a moth flutters on the surface in your
    morning tea
The rational mind stands firm looking this way and that as renegade
    electrons pillage the spectrum due south
Art galleries flutter and go out beneath the relentless surge of venture
    capital feeding commercial real estate the brittle meatless bones of
    enterprise architecture

Winged beasts are not enough we have located the broad swipe of
    Golgotha's forehead
If and when conjoin to form a commando unit now deployed somewhere
    over the border the electric train set up in the 50s garage
In a dream of pickup basketball I couldn't shoot for shit what does it
    mean?
Instead an exclamation reclaimed the sudden air a trial balloon went
    sideways the past tense was put on waivers tell me the story of your
    unwarranted demise
It seems more complicated when you pick up the pieces left over from a

night torn apart by ravens only to discover gray light where a tan
house had been
Sound is the signal so much more to say
Future packs of dogs roam the streets in an imagination of desk clerks
satisfied to be almost finished
We've only just begun and are almost dead while simply going about our
business in the middle of a forest watch light flash high above
The gray whale arches under and over there they have rules about things
like horses driving deeper into the wilderness the things we set up to
be normal
Particulate matter suffuses the everyday the long haul bracketed by
stones the super continental the flat aspect alone among the billions
of images

THE SOMETHING THAT COMES OUT OF NOTHING

First, nothing, then the something that comes out of nothing
Nothing turns out to be more interesting than this certain something
It is definitely something, but what it is is still a matter of conjecture
Some believe it to be the first in a series of somethings that will one day
      amount to something important
Others think nothing of it or think it nothing worth dwelling on
Or that it is all right as far as it goes but that nothing in the end will come
      of it
Most remain entirely unaware of it, buried as they are in the
      multitudinous signals that stream through their various devices
Nonetheless, whatever its ultimate fate, this something cannot be denied
      its moment
It leaves its mark to produce a kind of shuddering trail of reverberations
      as random passers by stop for a moment to regard it, quizzically at
      first, later with dawning recognition
This goes on for some time until eventually, through frequent
      association or blind habit, this certain something blends in with
      everything else to comprise the new nothing

FAMILIAR FACES UNDER SOFT LIGHTS

When in the course of humid vents
Pile the kids in the car and blow town
Put points on the board in order of appearance
Here clearly hear the sounds of the diners downstairs, the heater
    blowing morning air, the fictional buzz in the head joint
All you have can be summarized in two words: perfect binding
Flash of sky, second nature, parallel vision, string of beads, only child,
    where to?
You are held together by your reflexes

Billing periods life on a mountain top temperatures in the low 80s
How can you afford all these woods?
Whose words are these I think ye all evil
Until light spools from the mind of a mnemonist
Spread silently over the ocean floor
In time for a nap in tap shoes and a coke with you
Lights glimmer from across the Hudson in a poem by Paul Blackburn

In other words the world isn't going to wait for you any longer
Take comfort in standing bamboo
Familiar faces under soft lights
Home is where the harp is
When you wish upon a starter kit
Slather mustard liberally
While ring grabbers gobble up space

Whichever comes first is a funny way to look at something
The ordinary people outside the school in the morning
The leaf blowers grooming the business park
The traffic flows lighting up the map
A crow repeats itself quizzically
All spring breaks loose
Every story has a beginning, a middle and an interruption

Super soakers are really popular in the Midwest in August
Good morning, Addis Ababa!
While you row, row, row your bot Gentilly down the streaming media
Get a load of this one
Diary of a country wise ass
On and off all day the thermostat does its work the traffic lights play out
It would be marvelous to ride the whole length of the Missouri

The station agent will punch your ticket now
These letters inform us of our special mission, to fill in the cracks in the
    landscape
A special sizing glue is included in your composition plan
So you can decide where to eat lunch
Out in the yard or back in the truck
At evening the heat will dissipate
And the voices of kids rise up above the racket of skateboards

CONSTRUCTION IS THE NOISE OF SPRING

Any time zone will do
Wake up the toes
The stripper April Flowers
50s tabloid architecture
Rival unions in mid-air

Construction is the noise of spring
Walk to the beat
Squatters flock to empty office
The situation is vague
Neither of you has any change

Satisfactory household dice
The next door neighbor, the cousin, the kid
Something is alive oh metronome
The battle not shown on TV
Deep questions figure these hands

Watch your head
Memory is a flashlight
One standing at the rail of a ferry
The harbor thick with foam
Leaving or returning, which?

Voices, people
The whole bed turns over
Sounds of coffee fill the house
A clean design
A missing part

Then the impossible happens
Then and only then
The definite curve of time

Biting down on synchronicity
With an actor's intuitive claim

I haven't seen you in a long while
And don't see you now
Except in retrospect
The pronouns marching through the gate
In a steady drizzle

How stationary to be seated at a hotel room window
Overlooking Forest Park in Saint Louis
In 1967
As if for all time
Spread out before you

A kind of intimacy
That takes its time
From a map of the night sky
And turns it over
There is nothing on the other side

The self is like a wheel
Recollecting the invention of fire
A touch of work
A spray can
Spring colors

Wipe it all out and start again
Not the same person
Bearing scars and tattoos
Secure identity management
The dream of the modern mariner

Lines intersect to make a point
Branches branch out

Clouds obfuscate
The favela is alive
The beach is a line of prose

Any time zone will do
Construction is the noise of spring
Satisfactory household dice
Memory is a flashlight
Voices, people

Then the impossible happens
In a steady drizzle
As if for all time
There is nothing on the other side
The self is like a wheel

TIME IS WHAT WE ARE GIVEN

Time is what we are given
On any given day
Unless we have to work that day
Which is a great big *unless*
Since most of us work most days
Be that as it may
In which case what's time?
It's an open and shut case
Open to interpretation, eyes wide shush
Softly as in a morning after

I placed a glass of water in Berkeley
There was no time in it
The water that *is*
Place names mean everything
Even or rather especially if you never go anywhere
Such as Recife, Kyoto, Dakar, Churchill, Fort Benton or Seoul
By staying home such places are multiplied in thought
Thoughts of arugula, pepper, tomato and thyme
Cloud cover like a wet swim suit
Time is of existence

Workers of the word, unite!
Do you like to play around with predicates?
The world has plenty
They fit like a glove
On the myriad hands of time
How many of you are there?
Good question
One of us stayed behind at the last stop
To inspect the viticulture
Life on the vine is an open season

How lifelike the minimal alternate fonts of life!
Is that so surprising?
Sometimes nothing is
The nothing that *says*
The world and its chlorophyll basis
The shop floor ringed with sound
Sun on the pages of a book
The eyes go forward and back
Fossils crop up in the yard
Cross town on a mission to feed Bubbles

Be that as it may
Name something it appears to stay put
Place names mean everything
There is a world of shimmering glass days and a world of cold, forgotten
  days
The world has plenty
Like driving a grand piano through a keyhole
Is that so surprising?
The past is packed in ice
The future is already upon us
Breathe when ready

RELAXIN' AT YORKVILLE
for Nada Gordon

Roomlike interior
Life busting city
Glad to have time
After a while
Start to fidget
The outside of inside

Take your hands off
And walk to work
The bus poster professes
In the eye's mind
Any day of the week

Hands free high spirits
Eyes meet brick surface
Windows on soul food
Night in a paper cup

Ordinarily I'd be at my desk
Rearranging the deck chairs
On the Titanic
A white collar wanker
Brimming with haste
Which is nothing to sneeze at
Like dirt
And tells you you are alive
But today I am elsewhere
Relaxin' at Yorkville

Far off sirens
Remind us of life
It's an emergency

One emerges from the cave
It's too bright out
Everything is moving too fast

We take refuge in poetry
Balancing on the head of a pin
We zoom in on
Such that it flattens out beneath us

Over the edge of the metaphor
And far below
The landscape slides every which way

It is good to know
What you are talking about
We never do
Not entirely
Because the words got there first
Though we sometimes know more than we can say
The world and its streets, places

It's great to be with you
And it's great to be alone
Holding hands with the future
Even now it is upon us
Like a cheap suit
The first few drops of rain
A downpour for days

Do not stop until you reach
Edge of land
Step off planet
Wander empty stars
Smile at glimmer
Picture window open

Lend hand in case of need
Cut and paste across town
Lots of people to see
Curbside sensational glory

Do not stop until you reach
Life busting city
Even now it is upon us
In the eye's mind
It is good to know
Eyes meet brick surface
And far below
Like dirt
Far off sirens
We zoom in on

MISTAKES ARE NORMAL

You don't refuse to breathe do you?
Neither here nor there
Hear traffic from lobby
A former train terminal
Locomotive sticking out
In big old historical photo

Oops, wrong building
A typical mistake
Assuming entropic coincidence
Where there is none
Except in the eye of the beholder

Poet gets wires crossed
Crosses street to other building
Cloud business
Needs everything
Dear Old Stockholm

Some poems
Are air tight
Symmetrical chambers
Others sprawl
Roots dragging clods of earth
Loose ends
Teeming with microbes

When you hear something
Act right away
Why wait?
The drums of morning resound in the hills
Time to get busy
Life flies in the face of reasons

The lawn chair empties
Into the weekday morning
The dream locomotive
Pulls the melody into the roundhouse
Whose voice is that?
At last it comes to me
It is Hector Lavoe, La Voz
Explaining something in valiant rhyme
Across eons
Newly revealed in the pale light of day

Mistakes are normal
Dolphy built a system
Memory is like a cheese

Don't wait another moment
And while you're waiting
Consider this
This need to be heard
That's round and vibrant and unclassified as of yet

A turned over bucket for a table
Fragments of a life float forward
On wings of song
The turn of phrase is unimaginable in any other language
But this one, the language of stones
Obdurate integers in a steely calculus
That evaporates when you come to think of it

Books pile up
One meme, one tweet
Under God knows what

One thing happens
And then another
Ain't that just like it?
Arranged in lines
That tell a story
Or make a song
As long as the day is long

NO TIME LIKE THE RIGHT TIME

Fat beautiful things behind all these words
Juice of life
Salt in the waves that wound
Weather from another planet
Going to great lengths

Conversational snatches overheard
Concentrate on your thoughts
And the music sounds brighter
Coming as it does
From entirely somewhere else

Time goes away for a while
Somebody missed their connection
The sun blazes afresh
The count starts at one
And so on into inestimability

Our voice knows more than we do
Various things picked up over time
Might come in handy
The plain fact of having been there
Look away look back and see

No two ways about it
British Thermal Units
Versus Global Info Systems
A minor interval
Your regularly scheduled program

Flies in the face of all that sky
Leaves alive in summer heat
Generations that last

Play it the same way twice, thrice, force
Leave your hands at the door

The line has to be at least as long as
Songs are for the people
Poems for whoever's left over
There goes the train, freight
Such is your epochal moment

Algorithmic composites invent a world
Pain is really really real
Do what you have to do
Screen out so much other stuff
Wake up all over again

No time like the right time
Cool under cloud cover, sober
Mining contingency by the lake
What you learned being there
Putting the puzzle pieces together slowly

That's absolutely right
Acronym village, divestiture park
A data necklace
Birds of the northern climes
What does not repeat is a season of boundless delight

DREAMS ARE AS REAL AS WE ARE

Dreams are as real as we are
Have to buy more coffee at the store
We live in the future's past
Squiggly lines of our birth and sideways manner
Day templated by day
Birds and trains and traffic
Chug of instantaneous thought
Prize skin
Our endless immaterial youth
Having grown up between two pianos

The wealth of streets
Letters carved in a tree trunk
The trunk line is dream
After that they just keep adding cup holders
Haul ass across chasm
Zip up tornado
Promenade down Main Street
While fishermen hold flowers
It's the life of "Really?"
A question mark hanging from a balance beam

Welcome to the not yet
We've been expecting you
There is a constant turnover in the ranks of those who are sleeping
This medium is insanely great
Just enough to touch your toes
Air traffic control on steroids
Simply a matter of time
Thrown out on the fly
Able to leap tall buildings in a single bound
Standing still for long periods of time

I guess you could say we're working on it
Characteristic moves on the riddle rack
Recycle your pennies, friends
A roomful waiting for lift-off
The last day of school
Having agreed to meet
Like getting dressed in the dark
A taste unlike any other
At the end of the day
When all is said and done

Stand and/or deliver
Foibles of the currency exchange
Youth meets age at the crossroads
Occupation? As you see
Take off your head and relax
The sounds of landscaping rip through the tidal day
Breathe in a stroke of good luck
Fix your bike
The whole bay area is up for grabs
We have a rehearsal scheduled for every minute

FAR BE IT FROM ME
After Dave Morice

Far be it from me
To be bold 2.0
Poem as selfie
A movie theater is a big restaurant
A cigarette is a glass of milk

THE TURNSTILE OF THE PRESENT

The turnstile of the present
The momentarily revolving door
The past is too much information
The future nobody knows
Who grew up changing channels

WHERE HERE WE GRIND

Where here we grind against the order of events
Wake up into it – who am I?
The startling rip-off of ripe fruit
By clear-cut specialists
Separating one day from the next

You could say more if you took your mind off it
Scramble of mountains, rounds of lumber
Rents forcing trendy restaurants to close
The substitution of one bridge for another
Decks of equivalences dealt face down on the table

Silent numbers stand for the space between tries
Pull one book out the stack collapses
Eavesdropping media serve weakness at breakfast
Time travel isn't just for geeks anymore
Bootstrapping ridiculous speed

The tool works not because it's elegant
But because it gets us to hash things out
Travel and writing are the same
The shoulder moves in its harness
The airplane disappears over head

Do the dogs really think that's a rabbit?
Can you focus on one thing here for a minute?
Or does your attention deficit mandate a cavalcade of subjects
Each loosely coupled to the last?
A perpetual state of in-between-ness

There will be plenty of time to summarize the interview findings
And frame recommendations for moving forward
Hum of traffic an amalgam of intent

All we can say is we are in it
The way money, like language, changes hands

Take off your shoes and socks
Take everything off
Stand naked in the dawn light shifting forms from dark to bright
The wireless is upon us
Our thoughts a succession of electrical charges

You sent me a text and my phone buzzed next to you
I was in the other building
You brought it to me
Then it rang
I had spaced out my appointment

Patterns in the carpet always leaving a way out
They absent themselves from the pressing claustrophobia of time
We plan our exit strategy
Diligently hedging our bets
As the planet rolls up to the door of the sun

I must tell you this
There is so much I haven't said yet
The urgency factor is off the charts
When will I see you again?
What is the name for the difference between then and now?

IN MY GUISE

In my guise as a business person
As a musician, a poet
In my guise as a son, a husband, a Papi
My guise as a man
I glide in my guise
And the stars wheel in the sky
Have you noticed the days are getting shorter
Not really, it still stays light pretty late
Summer is an expanding form
In my guise as a watcher of days

The landscapers have arrived
In my guise as a homeowner
In Spanish they speak of the task at hand
The sound of the mower enters my poem
Communicating vessels pour information back and forth across the
    universe of forms
I go back over the story again and again
In my guise as a dreamer
One who imagines the world as it appears
Slightly modified each time wholly different suddenly transformed
Throwing light off in waves

The poem is a place to be for a little while
I enter in my guise as a reader
The words light up as my eyes pass over them
Each is a token of my affliction
I must be hung up on expression
The way a certain person sees and says what is going on for them
Fascinated I am in my guise as a riverboat captain
Surveying the banks in search of native life
The way things are now, were then
The highlights of a conversation opening paths into the future

I remain in place in my guise as a seated figure
Time runs through my fingers
Nothing is very convenient right now
Yet my health is good enough
In my guise as a normal animal
At noon I will take my leave
The sounds of transportation penetrate the open pores of the membrane
    of possible answers

What was the question?
A theme of instances flows against the shores of time
Open the black box of personality
Remove all parts
I can see where all this is going
In my guise as a trenchant observer
A blue jacket
A bemused attitude
A pair of legs
In my guise as none of the above

That things will be not only different but also more so
That unexpected eventualities will interrupt the proceedings
That messages will get mixed
That tremendous joy and love will be declared and concretely validated
That new meetings will give off authentic sparks
And even at night alone in the dark the wheel of life will continue to turn
Making the way more difficult, more interesting, more fully charged
So that whatever I say
In my guise as a village explainer
The drift of my words will be constantly exceeded by the manifold
    streamings of minutely colored cells

A TRANSOM WINDOW

A patient button
A struck match
A little paddle
A rent party
A delicious meaning
An ocean liner
A pool cue
A Ouija board
A claims form
A transom window

The connecting logic
The barking dog
The opposite reaction
The people beforehand
The great lesson
The lonely asterisk
The stated goal
The way back
The tiger shark
The still photo

Still listening
Wondering how
Sometimes hums
Run into it
Head around
Now in town
It gets away
Stay friends with
Limited time
More and more so

You have your way
An empty beach
The wind picks up
You know it
And in a moment
A car pulls up
We ought to be
For all we know
Similar to putting
Clasp hands

Less territory
Brilliant colors
Shades of Africa
Sun's the source
Wriggle into bed
Stride across
Where the land meets
And deeds are done
This offering I
Speaks out

Lesser of two
Air traffic condensation
A word to
And my blessings hence
Were I a traveling
Where the betters come from
It's perfectly insane
This bombardment
Undraw the lines then
The pattern slips off

Giant factory
Liminal seating

Part for whole
Universal joint
Arm in arm
Squarely in sites
Go about business
Of living the fruit
And best connection
Skipping down the late

THE LINE IN THE SAND

Trying to remember that song
The changes, so like that other one
That other singer, those other chords
A pattern recognizable only as such
In a wind of banter fastened to a length of sleep
The line extends for miles
The rockets fly up
Bombardment rains steadily down
We hold these truths to be self resident
If I could see it your way I probably would

We live in the gaps
Dash across street in hail of bullets
Of messages, texts, digits, beats
The information today is sizzling
How large are the holes for arms, body and head?
You have to sweat it out
This century's yet a teen
Constantly breaking out
Sullen, angry, horny, overwhelmed
Who put the my in front of life?

Compulsively checking the device
Longed for interruption, inexhaustible flow
We don't wear watches anymore
Stare at palm instead
An alternative flexion of the forearm
Focus on metrics, metadata, counters, forms
In relief against the urgency of that which must be done
According to whom?
And the streets unwind toward a limitless horizon
Where mind and body coincide

You have shoes on, have a heart
The kids at the border are only that
Or playing at the beach
Not yet branded with hatred
My dream a song sung across the century
Big wheels rolling along the changes
The man is in the cab
Dialectical onions
Let the woman take the wheel
A summary of body parts complete with map

Now get hundreds of channels, all bad
What would restore to earth its color
Before a word to the wild
Where summer opens the trap door to fucking off
Happy to be enveloped in fog
And read a delicious magazine full of air
With the monomania of a beetle
While friends conspire to launch hotels in fields
Never before entered
Such is the red in oblong samizdat payphones

The line in the sand is a mark soon lost to memory
We don't know yet who we may be
Scales are for snakes
Developers fishing for music
A wacked out sense of time as going both ways
What's happening now is more or less than enough
Monks chant in caves
Poetry is provincial, oppressed, rainy
People are mostly ok
The stream of life breaking the bank of language

THE POEM IS A REVERSIBLE JACKET

The poem is a reversible jacket
The sea flows backwards
Extravagant gestures end in the yellow of fennel
Wispy white clouds in a high bowl of infinite blue
Totemic prayer flags of our garden: wolf, raccoon, owl, mountain lion,
    frog, turtle, beaver, rabbit, snake
Hum of city streets
Leaves paint themselves onto the eyes

I would write a dream but am wide awake
The text slips aside in the breeze
The author is a machine
Jet noise a prolonged opening
One thing leaks to another
Before coming to light on a wire fence

DAYDREAMING IN ICELANDIC

He would have been 98 today
The apple doesn't fall far from the tree
The Newton
Personal display of affection
Reading his way off the farm
That you then have to turn around and be someone else
Characteristic stripes
Beginning in D minor
The color of sunburnt grass
Daydreaming in Icelandic

An urge to put all this away
Pushing forward into the 1940s
When all will be revealed
Out of the anechoic chamber of World War II
People to meet work to complete
Wind in the trees across a golden field
A personality a day
Getting out of the car and walking
The rhythm of life kicks in
Not sure if that's ever been said before in just that way

Light winds caress the planet
From this vantage point
The hand writes everything
The word everything
I'm only sleeping
A wooden mallet
Resting on a green pillow
What sense is this that rises up from the ground
Ripe for speculation
Star studded

The voice is a car
We are transported
His minute script
The page completely clothed in annotation
Words holding the world in check
Then an opening out
So something else can happen
A roll of the dice
Will never abolish chance
Call and response

WE KEEP SAYING THEY THOUGH SHE IS GONE
For Tom White, in memory of Leslie Scalapino

We keep saying they though she is gone
They have traveled a lot
They like wine
She likes rich colors
She would have been 70 today
Who had the courage of her convictions
Wrote in subjunctive voice to own the conditional nature of our
    existence
That they were at the beach
Waves forming and un-forming a steady stream of phenomena

A global sense of things that all bodies are related
Mind a shimmer in the engine room
Inhabiting genre with passport carefully in hand
Nights cold and a shiver of uncertainty
Dust from the road and ocean somewhere below
Place is neither here nor there
Voice a continuance
Woven of stories
As surveying a field of grass, a kind of yellow

Some small yellow wildflowers, buttercups?
Reality beckons, language pulls up short
Science demonstrates accurate description is possible
Propels engineering for better or worse
No going back
Yet here we can appreciate nature
For a few days
A sip of cold coffee
Feel of the sun

Being human remains coolish
Industrial agents read numbers in the book of days
We are only talking
The birds and fish go their separate ways
The air is bright, empty
Your hand on the page
A relation across space
The specificity an entry point going forward
A boat on the sea

She is off the earth
She is a citizen of life
The animal kingdom thrives nearly undiminished
The hawk wheels in the sky
Nothing is simple
Her works extend across the borderline of the century
The redwoods stand unabashed
Something helps this to be said
How very many life forms there are

THE DANDELIONS ARE OUT AGAIN THIS MORNING

The dandelions are out again this morning
In late afternoon they disappear
Must be the sun opens them
And in shade they silently close
A fog bank beyond the farthest line of trees
Hovers over unseen ocean
Fades imperceptibly into light blue

Here daisies grow wild by the porch
On long stalks that wave in the breeze
Leave well enough alone
An expression likely to recede
For we do not talk like that anymore
You know what I'm saying?
The fog advances now cloaking the tree line in mist

Birds cruise the fields
Three robins on the lawn hopping
Blue jay on a branch of pine
Sound track of calls most various
These are mere outlines of description
An embarrassment of sincerity
One giving oneself to place

In the shade of the porch the hum of the fan
A CD hung with fishing line twirls in the breeze
A signal to unwanted intruders, stay away
The wind picks up, coolness
Letters on a page in sun
Under shade of hand
Not satisfied, no, not ever

Sky completely empty overhead
Sun on neck and shoulder
Memory clasped in language
Moving across a field
Fog graying and drifting
Fawn enters field from forest
[...]

THE SKY IS WHITE BECAUSE IT'S FOG

The sky is white because it's fog
Stop explaining things
What you are doing is simply writing things down
The matter at hand is a form of expression
There's a bird now gone out the window

Life continues deep inside a redwood stump
Half covered in scrub
Comparisons, references, shrines
Deal with all that later
Come to find out at rest

Again the switching of implements
A red pickup kicks up dust
Something as close to nothing as something can be
Teeming with life on the surface
As a rock has a lichen coat

Anticipation, the signal thrill of
These blacks and yellows that you call friends
Meaning gets loose all over the place
Landing without a ladder
Strictly speaking not somehow dry yet

No change the sky is still white out
A tune ends, doors open and close
Right next to nothing there is that special something
Pry it loose from that rock
Hard to see why in these enclosures

Only that time has its hands on you
The ongoingness of it
As light causes shadows to appear

Bug taps window
Expectation that fog might lift

Substitution of day for night
Rotation of the earth
The planets secure in their orbits
The far reaches of space
Get in the car and go

By this time next year you will be entirely something else
We don't know the future
Words written down are what they are
Everything shifts slightly or ends up entirely otherwise
Nothing is as it is for very long

THE STAR INSIDE THE ROCK

No knock on namesake
Celebrity vibes
Caught up in folds of thought
History is relentless
No likelihood of neighborhood
Blue bottle fly by night stockings
Sovereignty is bat shit
The star inside the rock
Tunnels under the day
Down a green abyss
Wherein the planets lie lopsided
As many as you can tell
New information all the time
Changes the odds
Workshop of potential lit fuse

To give you first have to have
Next to a massive stone
Body mind at attention
Spirit bus pulling away
A person of appetites
Coastal trails in a light fog
Savagely falling asleep
A descender dropping down a whole line
As every utterance enters into exploration
Never will this mind of ours be still
Put on a hat and coat and boots
Trains of the westward ho
Coin enough to last
Belly up to the bar
Turn into something else

WALKING AND TALKING

Space to look out from
Rounding a curve
Ezekiel saw the wheel
It was way up there
This is the way we do it

Double back in sleep
The whole coast lit up from above
Mortal engine trouble
When were you in the service?
Conversation piece gas pump

Listen to no music
Breathing between lines
A point on a map
A plane in the sky
Continue nation

Get undressed
Take your head off
Climb out of your body
Merge with air
Be the temperature

Open to the elements
Sexually available light
Across the full spectrum
A paradise of shared beats
Keeping time alive

Walking and talking
That's about it
Remember to remember

Strokes for the folks
The stars our destination

When in the course
Light on olive tree
How many leave takings
How many leaves
It's a wide wide word

That roads out from nowhere
Stops along the way
Made breakfasts
Covered wagons
Sleek schooners

Time intervenes
It's not unusual
The map is not terrible
The lines nicely bent
Everything happens for a season

Use what's close at hand
The instruction set
Sun rises into the sky
Business as usual
Normally be here by now

WHAT A BEAUTIFUL THING

What a beautiful thing
Madison Bumgarner and Bob Dylan on the same night
Flicker of phones at the Paramount
And good news about a cure
And missing sunglasses
We check at Plum Bar, nope
Then in the car, yep
At intermission
As the crow flies
As you were saying

Simple statements of fact
Persist in the mind's eye
When no one is looking
A length of pipe
A frontage road
A pair of fuzzy dice
She keeps telling her son to put more things in his poems
Mind the color of a sidewalk
Mind the gap
A hundred cars lined up to cross the bridge

One never knows, do one?
Darkness at the break of noon
The crow caws from the tree
Consumer-grade simplicity
Stuff is very valuable
Have to be available
What time will you be home?
Say so soon enough
Get caught up with all that stuff
In the barnyard of daily life

Hands on hips
Loss of life and limb
Carrier pigeon
Aerial shot
It seems like only yesterday the mail arrived
Life on the line is bad
A character actor
Climbing into a station wagon
At dawn
What were you thinking?

Not much is happening
Blood runs hot
Take a breather
The newspaper no one remembers
Door slightly ajar
In between time is the right time
A paean to distraction
Concentrated flute jook
Alternating current
He's got the whole world in his hands

Come to think of it
The comfort zone
Way out on the prairie
Lights out speed
Solid command
Family practice
Perfect pitch
The way it seems
And the way it is
That's what I love about the South

INTERNAL COMBUSTION

Internal combustion
Clairvoyant journalist
See and be seen
Fantasy cocktails
Hang by a thread
A nip in the air
Duly noted
Don't be silly
Have a heart
The train leaves the station
You're going to need stitches

It isn't easy
Compulsory arbitration
Re-doing the reports
A midnight walk
By the water's edge
Ceremonial shopping cart
Goth lamppost
The shadow of your smile
Lyric monuments to flight
Caught in the net of all seeing

Abracadabra
Remarkable flutter
Captions are very dear
Hope you can make sense of
Gave up a long time
Over into under
As to where to go from
Before it's late enough
And you can sleep
Standing up walking and being on

Engineering degree centigrade
Imaginary drinks
You cannot be serious
Said and done travel
A noon bath
Modern time
Alphabet suit
Neither here nor there
Formerly known as touch
We wish only to connect the dots

FOR SELLING CIGARETTES?

What is the grand jury selection process?
What tube or tune do you think in?
An open road
No traffic
Gliding over mountain contours
Like Bob Grenier's *Day at the Beach*
A return to the known
Replenishing scratch of day
Not ever entirely the same
Periods of heavy rain

For selling cigarettes?
The dream channel is a slender band
Conservative attempts to enforce one-way traffic
Choke hold on signification
A culture of fear
Ten orange tulips
Slip into something more comfortable
The map is not the territory
We been here before
The heating guy is here

How many deaths will it take till he knows?
History is a nightmare
Wake up from your nap
And go to the refrigerator
Women and children have been living life all along
What is up is a question of standing
The rumble of garbage cans wheels on wet concrete
One word plastic a movie past perfect
Hannah Weiner said, "It's a pleasure to meet a fellow bi-lingual"
We live in it and it keeps going

The filter is completely shot
Plane noise more than it lets on
Contact your particulars
Neither a sandwich nor a soup spoon be
Yet nestle in a terry cloth robe
Today's date is within budget
My Mom commented on my status
The planet will be closed for repairs
Someone coming down stairs
Turning back into work and sleep

Is it ok if we live and breathe?
The streets have a crumpled look like a cup of coffee
On a park bench
A stop-and-go move can shake a defender and score from downtown
It isn't what you think
Day has wheels drivers don't even feel the road with
Armatures of flight
Escape routes for the soul
Gathering music up in our arms
We need to wake up and change shit

LANE SHIPPING
for Ted Greenwald

Who is home when he is there?
Do his own shirts smell the best?
Is there room in the room that he rooms in?
Where is Snowden?
Do you have a license for that thing?
Windows on the weather
Sentinel dogs
Trade routes open the century
Interest groups vie over legalities
Here I lie among the flowers

We're going to be here for a while
Freedom's just another word
Adding to the enormous burpdom of words
We would have to have quiet time
In a cold, rain-soaked trench
Reading a detective book
By flashlight
Lane shipping
Load balancing
Container freight

What I have seen and heard already seems destiny
A singer with a voice like the great outdoors
Standing half open in a light drizzle
Turn on, tune in, trade route
I've half a mind
Celebrity judges on their way to the airport
You practice every time you pick up your instrument
Conflicting signals
She stayed the night
A dream is another story

Pain now will give pleasure later
That's what they say
A pronoun is a glass of milk
Up to the waist in mud
How do you say waterfront?
No word for what you have in mind
To balance memory and the immediate future
Which is to say the unknown
It is important to drift off to sleep

How much not enough is enough?
If we do this every day will we make progress?
Does she put on a different outfit every day?
Or just have one good one and really make it count?
Who is he when he's at home?
The heater clicks on when it's chilly
The calendar is not the year
The noise from the schoolyard is a sign of like
"Ever over" sounds like "even Steven"
Night riders stop for supplies at 7-11

A STONE'S THROW

A lake in a scene of totals
Going outside in the not rain
Being told it's this
What do you think of that?
Decided long ago to be out of it
Fairly long ride back
Limited time offer
Lost jobs doing years
Angular increments of patchy moss
A stone's throw

Irritable reaching for the next text
When light goes up on the mountain
You miss as much and return half vacant
Wet from sleep
Counter top enthusiasm
Signal summary news
Radio silence
Saying something off the beaten track
Especially when not even there
How many times have I told you?

Local color baked in
Only to forget
When sweeping the stones
In an imagination of morning
Stiff from sleep
Unable to carry a tune
Running out of think
A silent bidder in the auction house of time
Light and shadow in stillness
Breathing easier now

Sample foot display
Turn off heat
Instructions to the head
Make of day a pattern inside out
Retain the ridge line
Standing on ceremonial ruins
Drinking from a clay cup
Wishing to be otherwise
Wishing to be the same
Stand up and walk to the door

LIKE BIRDS IN AIR

The birds like to congregate on that platform
Language is a depot of spare parts
The feeling of having taken flight
The feeling when your flight is canceled
Shore birds classified by movable type

Between smoke and steam lies the difference
An unconscious delta where the stream of life gives out
Into the Gulf of Texaco
We should know better and we do
But only on certain days

Noir conjunctions mix birds up with platform light
Tree habits draw wires across fencing
The diagram of a chair
Light enters other color
When clouds skim in the sky

Now that the shadow has been broken
We are free to come out on the other side
Or would that be a retreat
From a recognition of non-freedom?
The reassembled shadows of language?

Succulents in winter
Birds and the hock of the metronome
Ripples on the surface of the bay
Sky reflected in a backwater
Nails coming out of the boards of the deck

Like birds in air, fish in water
There is no end to
Rolling out of bed

Putting one foot in front of
Sound of car on road

When you think you can't
And the mind tips upside down
Something else happens
As in a scale
There are places to land

Attracted to the fish
Just under the surface
The birds skim the surface or sit and float
A line of black figures along the platform
That someone built

Water pulling back, revealing sand
An arm of earth
That loves water, loves sky
Has ages of experience
Our green mother

The feeling of having been
But only on certain days
The diagram of a chair
Sound waves ripple the surface
There is no end to

EVERY TIME WE SAY GOODBYE

Winter light on the Pacific coast
You are way behind
Thanks, Hannah
Territory crisscross memory sample technique
A method to its madness
As when clocks wind down
Similar to swimming in summer

Thought is endlessly embodied
In the small of the back
Shoulder to the wheel
Hip thrust outward
In time to the music
Of a previous century
A long line of light-weight thinkers

Jam from that plum tree back there
Life is multitenant
We use the same codes to accomplish different tasks
A year to replace the broken one or two
Now on back order
Prayer flags line the interior of the skull
The congee seems to last forever

Every time we say goodbye
You have to back the car out of the driveway
This morning light from the east
Throwing color against the fence
Radio traces
Crushing jumbled chords into bricks
Hats of Iggy Azalea

It might be more it might be less
Anything can enter into it
Nothing is simple
Everything can be called by a different name
Theory of whatzit
You carry your demo on your back
Revolving doors neither open nor close

When you get to where you can see out
A kind of ecstasy
A sentence is something that completes itself
A phrase calls for more
A word is a unit of measure like a heartbeat
Pop no pills
We are about to be somewhere else or so it seems

The gradual drift of import heaves into view
From LA to Tokyo
One wants it to be something about sharks
She goes off to get ready
The air is alive with possibility
Recent experience has been awesome
Stay tuned for a long walk

RASPBERRIES IN JANUARY

Raspberries in January
Wall of chartreuse
Cannot land a punch
The presiding spirit of this dream cris cheek
Driving down to Louisiana
Fertile crescent of the west
Will POTUS veto the XL Pipe?

The nation state has had its day
Now we have global capital vs. Islamic jihad
It's not that simple
Voices echo deep within a cave
And do not stop to think if ever we return
We'll drink a cup of kindness
Oranges scattered in shade

Free union
Then return of the problem-solving mind
Regarding the stage plot
Where to put the speaker
Stop
Don't solve the problem
The problem will solve itself

Confirmed by the 10,000 things
Constantly in motion
Theater of operations
Studying for a final
If a lion could speak
A ship out on the sea
My life with the hour-glass turned over

Just walk away Renée
The sound of the 60s
Nostalgic even then
As youth mourns childhood's end
Time and time again
An idiomatic expression
In an idiotic age

When lizards grow feathers
Sky clouds over
Temperatures drop
World goes hurtling through space
Put affairs in order
Dress casually
Order chow mein to bring home

The light at the end of the tunnel
Is light green
There are no wrong notes
Only a few conventioneers and tourists drinking quietly
The kids call scare quotes "scrunchy peace"
We join the animals
It is a pleasure to say the least

UNCONFIRMED REPORTS

Long periods of silence
Random noise of earth effects
Simple misunderstandings
A serious painter in the traditional mode
Cats kick up clods of dirt
The train stretches toward the terminus
You have arrived exactly nowhere
A stray dot appears above your name in the winter sky
Let me know if there's anything I can get you
Sympathetic vibrations

Unconfirmed reports
Unanswered letters
Boots of Spanish leather
Weather patterns shifting over time
Put solidarity here, identity is over there
Noise is a by-product
Here is where you put in your time
A mad poet in a spring shift
The sentence pre-supposes a period
Earthworms aerate the soil

Male elephant seals rest for three months before mating
Lost emails
The phrase sounds familiar
No answer is the new no
A born musician on a permanent bandstand
Translations that surpass the originals
Understanding that every utterance could be the very last
Emotional climate overcast with occasional showers
Meaning is construction work
The message is addressed to all of you

MASTER CLASS
after Arnold Newman

Go ahead and call your people
The figure rises out of the ground
Confusion stamps a void across Europe
Winds of change swirl about the planet
Orange, green, white, purple, brown
As seen from space in NASA satellite time-lapse
Reminiscent of Allen Ginsberg

A landscape by Milton Avery
Be sure to bring water and a snack
Billions of particles moving every which way
A profound face, intricate depth of field
Weather patterns we live in, around and under
Debt slave revolt going on in Greece
Hyperlinks sensitize the websphere

Comments appear in quotes
Martha Graham in her studio
Austerity the grim mask of global banking
Tired after school
Our best intentions constantly interrupted
Pandemonium of all free spirits
Noon, hour of the smallest shadow

10:52, the sound of steps on the stairs
Flat descriptive prose over time
Body language tellingly tender
Jean Arp peaking out from behind a curved form
What is continuous? What is occasional? What lost? What found?
Let's go back and see what we have
Energized from dreams of anxiety, guilt and shame, the writing of them
    down

Terror of cracks in the pavement
Thursday, the downward slope
Festival of the oligarchs
Love in the alley
An opening in the fence
The fabulous vertical stripes of Diana Vreeland
Check your answers at the door

The non-stop fabrication of readymades
Compulsive hand-washing by executive order
Lisette Model and Berenice Abbott eye to eye
Copying jazz charts for rehearsal tonight
Momentarily off the hook
Sound vernissage
Fucking is out of this world

Talking is something we just do
The neighbors are restive
Shadow play of instants
Active verbs take time off to care for relative pronouns
Who grew up switching channels
Duchamp pointed sideways
Looking at pictures in search of the perfect subject

THE AVENUE OF KISSES

The nation state is history
Religion is an oath
Freedom of the press is for owners only
The mind is of two minds
The world is late for work

Diseases populate continents
Drugs are synthetic profits
Wait times may vary
In a broken cup
Tireless expeditions make landfall

Sadness and snow make drifts
Attention wanders
Alarms interrupt the proceedings
Police officers gather for coffee
Military miniatures arrive by mail from Europe

The moment of meteors has not yet come
There aren't many days left for sleeping
Puns recall songs without lyrics
Tyranny of languor
Time tied to a tree

Academic occupations in five-star hotels
The avenue of kisses
There is so much to be read in these passages
Days pass each other coming and going
Travelers emerge from dark forest to bright sandy beach

Less is more, there are those that say
Serious trouble is a given
Our laughter relates to the stars

The sun at night
A dream stem of heartfelt thanks

AN OLD SIGNATURE
for Bill Berkson

On my 1966 edition of *Lunch Poems* an old signature
Which is to say a young one
Testifies to pride of ownership
Then, suspicion of petty larceny
Given the imprint Pocket Poets

I'm old enough now to have been his father
When he wrote "The Day Lady Died"
Or even, in fact, when *he* died
So it's ok, I guess, that I drink a lot less
As life slips out the door and onto night streets
As I am still guarding it from mess and measure

Numberless birds and fishes I vow to awaken with
Make of air and water an unlimited home
Where what goes around comes around
And light enters the picture
A patron saint on a banana leaf
Suspended in space

You do the math
While I pack up these boxes
Destination, the stars my
Contents may shift
Address unknown (Elvis)

I wonder what Ron Padgett is doing right now
Probably looking out his window
At a gigantic snow drift in Vermont
And thinking of fixing lunch
Is it broken? Probably not
And anyway it's early here in California

Where I ply my quote unquote trade

I wouldn't trade it for a month of Sundays
A land bridge
A dream lodge
A suspended sentence

Plywood used to be used to shore up a foundation
Now we just tilt up the whole she-bang
Then go about our business
Doing detail work on contemporary reversible conveyances
Until the sun settles back behind rain clouds
And the deluge prepares itself for our astonishment

Once again the trees carelessly align
With a feeling for leaving
Of everything said in a day
Friendship, estuary, nut-and-bolt, feed lot
Paths crossed out
Appeals to log logic
Until the whole stands in for the part
Where the subject breaks down in tears
And rains wash the city
In time for its new lease on life

Several centuries worth of conversation later
I'm still doing the numbers
On my fingers
Hand in hand with fate
Or is it destiny?
I can never remember the answer
But you have to like this weather
Wet like earth
In the mind of a worm

On we go
You're all right in my book
The word stands for the thing
The thing falls over
We kneel down to pick it up
All lips and teeth
Alive to the noise of the generator

STARS OVER MONGOLIA

Books had fallen from the shelf
A kind of soothsayer
Capital Y for yes
Hung up in the storm drains
City of Paris
Closed for repairs
Two steps forward one step back
A lot of steps for a centipede
Straining after commentary
Where the wide things are

Time is a warm bath
Sign in using an assumed name
Be there for them
The radio tuned to space
Reading the signals from memory
In the fingers
The bones of the clock
Friday temperature perfectly natural weirdo
All is by my side
Now arriving at Gate 15

The true test is backing out
Something else will happen
Alive to the imprecision of it
My dream a coffee with Dante
Virgilian shivers
Everything that is true about today
Has been recorded on half-inch reel-to-reel
We're all making it all up anyway
According to Fichte
By way of Penelope Fitzgerald

Action is a golden sweater
Place stones on the back and legs
Your fantasy has shipped
Are those lines mountains or waves?
Time slips through our figures
Come back to bed
The day is arrayed transversely
Each earthling enters into earnest engagement
Stars over Mongolia
As clear and bright as serum

The life of a sign is internal
The wind cries many
Waterfall I tell you listen here
That sports its life in drops that shatter quietly
Seeming to be
What does not change is a festival
In full winter sum
The eyes are planets
That close to avert the sun
And open on stars only numberless

WEATHER
for Bob Perelman

Experimental subjects float upstream
Don't throw the baby out with the bathysphere
The blue collar devotion of the Larry Smith fan club
The rainbow jumper of Purvis Short
Jailbreak your device
Nothing bad happens
On the other side of the tracks
Lies the university
You must walk there dreaming of coal

Tip the cars over as if they were sitting ducks
Prosody is belts *and* suspenders
A little sobriety goes a long way
China is hardly schizophrenic
To write turn on the bathroom light
You're keeping us up
Yes we do still have paper
It is nothing to sneeze at
The weather is mostly air

By sleeping with art for many years
You have invented a new color
Which you call "left of blue"
Imagine a place on earth
Where the sky is like a sail
Spread over many quarters
Teeming with various life
And still not separate from itself
Let this be a listening to

Between night and day hangs a torn curtain
Let a hundred camels contend in the courtyard

The prison house of language is opening its gates
Pandemonium of all free spirits
Andre Iguodala to the rim
Two-thirds of the world's surface is covered with water
It must feel good
Timing is anything

THE LOST STEPS

Wait for the signals to drain
Then turn the devices back on
The twitter of birds is really real
Wake up and hear the coffee
Dear Finance
I hope you will pay me
Signs and waves

At the end of the day
A feeling of sadness
Mind all tired out
The lost steps
The uselessness of balconies
Sky going mauve in an instant
Let's drink a toast in a book

A boat out on the sea
My first one
Eager to get going
Taking everyone's feelings into account
Not at all easy
Too good to be true
Casting off from the dock

At the appointed hour
You are who you are at any moment
Who you happen to be
An extension in space and time
Rhyming with a conception
That sounds like but isn't your name
You who have always been so vital

An arranged silence
Communication from beyond the door
Father, mother, township, country, tribe
Popeye the Sailor
A thought, just had a
Borne along on the breeze

Stepping down from the bus
Sitting here in limbo
Some help from my friends
A day like any other
Hard to put a number on it
Can't wait to see
Each has a completely different perspective on what is going on

A novel is a landscaped park
The bottom line is a false front
Brilliant blue at the outset
The healing process takes time
From one window hangs the flag of an aspiring state
Walking through hotel corridors
The kingdom of this world

Name and address
Two verbs in one act
To get into total body control you have to call in early
Machine learning is old hat
Dear friends
A dog is barking in my neighborhood
I send you my deepest regards

THE ROSE QUARTET

Find quite amusing but don't know if really true
Late spring wisteria shave and go
Hold up your days for all to see
Riding bike into sudden snow
Coming up the rear
What is, under pressure from what isn't, or what isn't yet
A name by any other day would last a week

Large inventions surge forward
The layabouts lounge in the shade
Their laughter is like an unpaid bill
Every day is everybody's birthday
The debt load a mounted police
Time to be off
You can have my hats and coats

For a man to write as a woman
Requires imagination
The lighter of many fires
What voice would then resound in the head?
Neither a borrower nor a lender be
And forgive us our debts
A list as long as your arm

Somewhere off the coast a radio signal
Stopping by the woods to check email
And whether we get out of this in time is up for grabs
For stationery think envelope
For stationary think arrested adolescent
Poetry is news that has to stay after school
Leaf shapes that spell the velvet hammer

A long line of ancestors at the post office
The most important thing is to relax
Now you see it
The rose quartet
Barely stirring
In a light breeze
It's all right

Time opens onto a wide array
Today a trip to the city for lunch with Bill
You go your way past the algorithm mine
Drop names from tall buildings
Listen for bounce
Telling me just what a fool I've been
Imagination enters in terror, flowers in spring

One bad grout and the new Bay Bridge has to be done over
The taste is of pomegranate with a hint of machine learning
Everything that could be said shall be said
What counts is today
Making room for the centuries
Not something you consume, rather it consumes you
Who bears life has the last word

Photo by Alan Bernheimer

Kit Robinson is the author of *Determination* (Cuneiform, 2010), *The Messianic Trees: Selected Poems, 1976—2003* (Adventures in Poetry, 2009), and 20 other books of poetry. His collaboration with Ted Greenwald, *A Mammal of Style* (Roof, 2013), was named among "the best poetry of 2014" by the *Chicago Tribune.* He is a coauthor of *The Grand Piano: An Experiment in Collective Autobiography, San Francisco, 1975—1980* (Mode A, 2006—10). Robinson lives in Berkeley, works as a marketing consultant for cloud startups and plays *tres* guitar in the Afro-Cuban sextet Calle Ocho.

Made in the USA
Monee, IL
07 July 2026

56551610R00079